Next Time You See a
SEASHELL

BY EMILY MORGAN

National Science Teachers Association

Arlington, Virginia

NSTA Kids
National Science Teachers Association

Claire Reinburg, Director
Jennifer Horak, Managing Editor
Andrew Cooke, Senior Editor
Wendy Rubin, Associate Editor
Agnes Bannigan, Associate Editor
Amy America, Book Acquisitions Coordinator

ART AND DESIGN
Will Thomas Jr., Director

PRINTING AND PRODUCTION
Catherine Lorrain, Director

NATIONAL SCIENCE TEACHERS ASSOCIATION

Gerald F. Wheeler, Executive Director
David Beacom, Publisher

1840 Wilson Blvd., Arlington, VA 22201
www.nsta.org/store
For customer service inquiries, please call 800-277-5300.

Lexile® measure: 810L

Special thanks to Dr. José Leal, director of the Bailey-Matthews Shell Museum in Sanibel, Florida,
for reviewing this manuscript.

Library of Congress Cataloging-in-Publication Data

Morgan, Emily R. (Emily Rachel), 1973-
  Next time you see a seashell / by Emily Morgan.
    p. cm.
  ISBN 978-1-936959-15-0 (print) -- ISBN 978-1-936959-73-0 1. Mollusks--Juvenile literature. 2. Shells--Juvenile
literature. I. Title.
  QL405.2.M665 2012
  594--dc23

2012027770

To my mother, Vonda Stevens,
for teaching me that seashells don't have to be
perfect to be beautiful.

"If a child is to keep alive his inborn sense of wonder, he needs the companionship of at least one adult who can share it, rediscovering with him the joy, excitement, and mystery of the world we live in."

—Rachel Carson

A NOTE TO PARENTS AND TEACHERS

The books in this series are intended to be read with a child after he has had some experience with the featured objects or phenomena. For example, give your child a seashell or a handful of seashells and encourage him to observe them and wonder about them. Talk about where they might have come from. Share stories about a time you went to the beach or found a fossil of a shell. Ask what he is wondering about the shells and share what you wonder. Then, with shells in hand, read this book together and discuss new learnings. You will find that new learnings often lead to new questions. Take time to pause and share these wonderings with each other.

This book does not present facts to be memorized. It was written to inspire a sense of wonder about ordinary objects and to foster a desire to learn more about the natural world. My favorite question from students after giving them a handful of shells to observe is, "Are these real?" I think they ask that question because seashells look like pieces of fine art that a person carefully sculpted and painted.

Children are naturally fascinated by seashells, and when they contemplate the fact that these beautiful shells are made by slimy, snaily mollusks, the shells become even more remarkable. My wish is that after reading this book, you and your child feel a sense of wonder the next time you see a seashell.

—Emily Morgan

Next time you see a
seashell, pick it up and
hold it in your hand.
Run your fingers over it.

Does it feel smooth
or rough?

How would you
describe its shape?

What colors or
patterns do you see?

Is it dull or shiny?

Smell it.
Does it have a scent?

What words would you
use to describe the shell?

Seashells are some of the most beautiful objects found in nature. Have you ever wondered where they come from?

Mollusks! They are the shell makers. Mollusks are animals with soft bodies, such as snails, oysters, and clams.

Shell-making mollusks hatch from eggs.
Some mollusks lay their eggs in cases to
protect them. Sometimes you can find
these egg cases washed up on the beach.

If you look inside a mollusk egg case, you might see hundreds of teeny tiny shells. That's because these mollusks begin growing their shells very early in life.

If you find a shell that looks like half of it is missing, it's probably a bivalve. Bivalve shells have two parts connected by a hinge. When the mollusk dies, the two pieces usually come apart. Sometimes you can find the two pieces still attached, but be careful because they break apart easily.

The other main type of seashell is a gastropod. Unlike a bivalve shell, a gastropod shell is made of only one piece and often has a spiral on the end. Look in the opening of a gastropod shell. That's where the mollusk was attached.

Mollusks' shells help them survive. When a bivalve is startled, it quickly snaps its two-part shell closed, sometimes pushing out a stream of water to propel it away from danger.

When a gastropod is disturbed ...

it retreats inside its shell for protection.

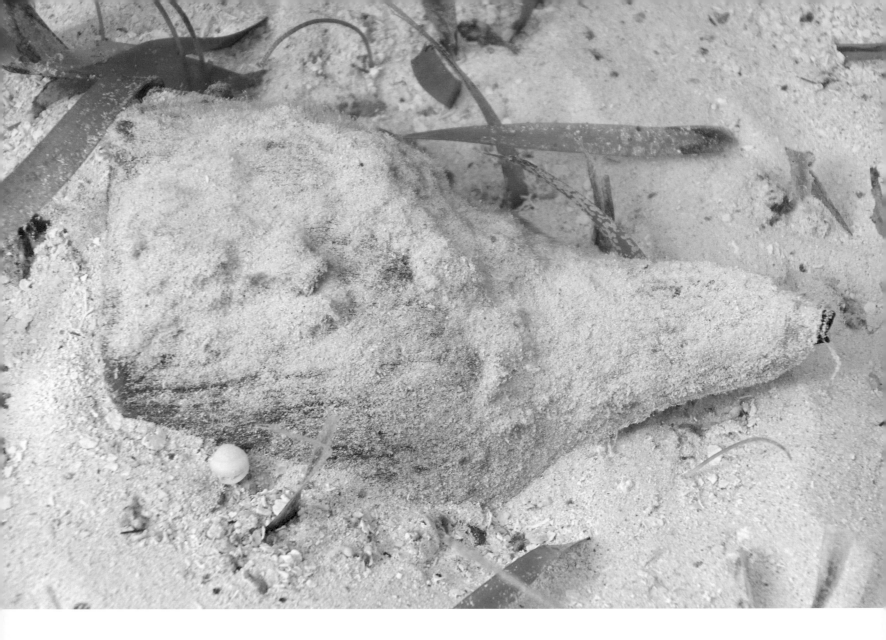

Some mollusks have colors or patterns on their shells that help them blend in with their surroundings. Sometimes the shape of a shell can help the mollusk bury itself in the sand to hide from predators.

You can learn about the life of a mollusk by looking at its shell. Cracks and chips might be clues about a battle with a predator. Small holes may have been made by an animal drilling into the shell to eat the mollusk. The colors of a shell can be the result of what the mollusk ate or the substances in the water where it lived. Some shells even have evidence that another animal lived on the shell.

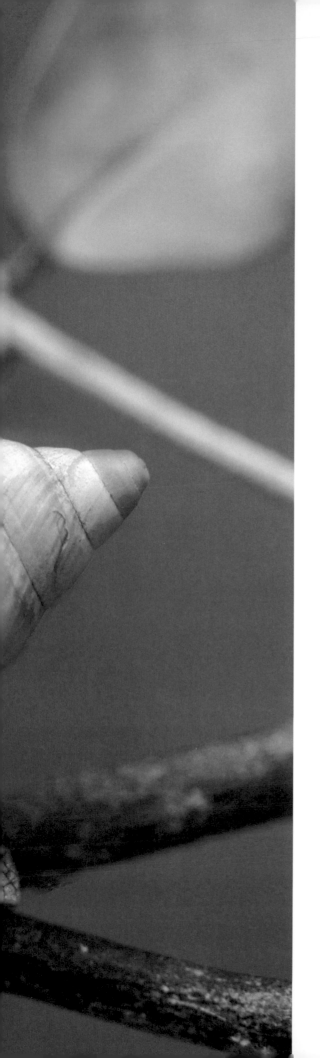

Beaches are not the only places where you can find shells. They can be found anywhere shell-making mollusks live: streams, lakes, or even forests.

Not all mollusks make shells. Slugs, squid, and octopuses are mollusks, but they do not make shells.

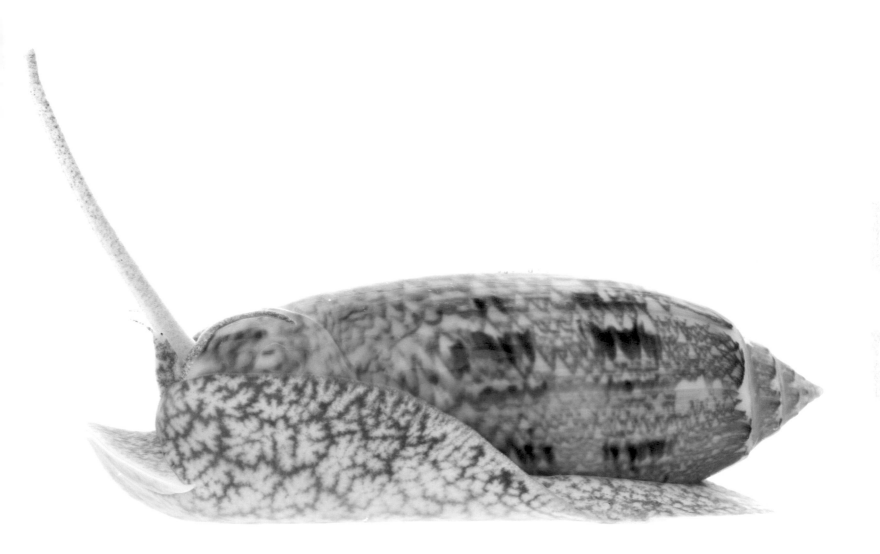

Some people think of a shell as a mollusk's home, but it is actually part of the animal's body. If you find a seashell that still has a live mollusk attached, leave it where you found it. Don't try to separate the mollusk from its shell. It will not survive.

You may have seen a hermit crab inside
a seashell. Hermit crabs are not mollusks.
They do not make shells. Hermit crabs use
empty mollusk shells to protect their soft bodies,
finding bigger shells as their bodies grow larger.

So the next time you see a seashell, remember that beautiful shell was made by a mollusk. It began as a tiny shell that hatched from an egg and grew with that mollusk to be the shell you now hold in your hand. Isn't that remarkable?

ABOUT THE PHOTOS

Calico scallop shell
(Judd Patterson)

Handful of gastropods
(Katie Hosmer)

Looking for seashells
(Katie Hosmer)

Observing a gastropod shell
(Katie Hosmer)

Pile of Florida seashells
(Judd Patterson)

Florida horse conch emerging
from its shell
(Seth Patterson)

Whelk egg case washed up on the beach
(Judd Patterson)

Peeking inside an egg case
(Katie Hosmer)

Lightning whelk shells
(Seth Patterson)

Sunray Venus shell attached at hinge
(Judd Patterson)

Live conch hiding in its shell
(Judd Patterson)

Bivalve shells and gastropod shells
(Seth Patterson)

Open and closed
Atlantic bay scallops
(Seth Patterson)

Banded tulip emerging
from its shell
(Seth Patterson)

Banded tulip retreating
into shell
(Seth Patterson)

West Indian chank camouflaged in the sand
(Judd Patterson)

Hole in a scallop shell
(Judd Patterson)

Liguus fasciatus, a tropical tree snail
(Judd Patterson)

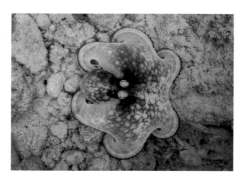

Caribbean reef octopus
(Seth Patterson)

Caribbean reef squid
(Seth Patterson)

Lettered olive
(Seth Patterson)

Caribbean hermit crab
(Judd Patterson)

Holding a gastropod shell
(Katie Hosmer)

Listening to a shell
(Katie Hosmer)

ACTIVITIES TO ENCOURAGE A SENSE OF WONDER ABOUT SEASHELLS

❖ Take a handful of shells and sort them into groups of your choosing (e.g., color, size, and texture).

❖ Sort a group of shells as bivalves and gastropods.

❖ Find several shells of the same kind, and compare them to one another. Talk about why the sizes and colors of the seashells might be different, even though they are made by the same kind of animal.

❖ Choose a shell to draw or paint, paying close attention to the colors and patterns.

❖ Choose a favorite shell to display in your home or classroom.

❖ Make a list of questions you have about mollusks. Do some research to find the answers.

❖ Hold a shell up to your ear. Listen as the shell amplifies the noises around you. What does the sound bouncing around in the shell remind you of?

WEBSITE

"The Secret Lives of Seashells" Video Clips From the Bailey-Matthews Shell Museum
http://shellmuseum.org/education/mollusks_video.cfm

Downloadable classroom activities with student pages can be found at
www.nsta.org/nexttime-seashell.

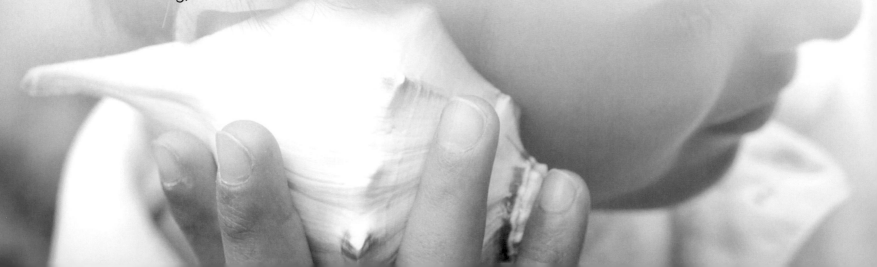